COUNTRIES IN OUR WORLD

INDIA

Darryl Humble

W
FRANKLIN WATTS
LONDON • SYDNEY

D0264740

Teddington Library

First published in 2009 by
Franklin Watts
338 Euston Road
London NW1 3BH

Franklin Watts Australia
Level 17/207 Kent Street
Sydney NSW 2000

Copyright © Franklin Watts 2009

All rights reserved

Produced for Franklin Watts by
White-Thomson Publishing Ltd
+44 (0) 845 362 8240
www.wtpub.co.uk

Series consultant: Rob Bowden
Editor: Sonya Newland
Designer: Hayley Cove
Picture researcher: Amy Sparks

A CIP catalogue record for this book is available
from the British Library.

Dewey Classification: 915.4

ISBN 978 0 7496 8844 8

Printed in Malaysia

Franklin Watts is a division of Hachette Children's
Books, an Hachette UK company

www.hachette.co.uk

Picture credits
Corbis: Cover (Jon Hicks), 9 (Frédéric Soltan/
Sygma), 12 (Jeremy Horner), 13 (Derek Hall/
Frank Lane Picture Agency), 16 (Bagla Pallava),
21 (Brian Lee), 23 (Phillipe Lissac/Godong), 24
(Stringer/India/ Reuters), 25 (Salvatore di Nolfi/epa),
29 (Michael S. Yamashita); **iStock:** 11 (Marshall Bruce);
Photoshot: 4 (Jean Chung), 14, 15 (Vishal Shah),
19 (World Pictures), 26 (WpN/UPPA), 27 (Xinhua);
Shutterstock: 6 (P. Borowka), 7 (Jeremy Richards),
8 (Regien Paassen), 10 (Salamanderman), 17 (Luciano
Mortula), 18 (Dana Ward), 20 (Jeremy Richards),
22 (Salamanderman), 28 (Syed Sajjad Ali).

Contents

With more than 1.1 billion people, India has the second largest population in the world after China. Indian culture and beliefs have influenced other countries for centuries, but recently it has been India's rapidly growing economy that has made it globally important. India is now set to become a new economic superpower.

▼ *Shopping malls like this have become a symbol of modern India, but they reflect the widening gap between rich and poor.*

Mixed benefits

Not everyone in India is benefiting from the changes that are taking place. About a quarter of the population (almost 300 million people) live in poverty. This is especially noticeable in India's cities, where people may not have a home and instead have to live on the streets. For these people life is very different from that of India's growing middle classes, who enjoy a good standard of living, with modern homes, cars and enough money to enjoy shopping and entertainment. Fixing this divide between the 'haves' and 'have-nots' in India is one of the country's greatest challenges for the future.

AFGHANISTAN

Indus River

C H I N A

P A K I S T A N

Delhi

New Delhi ■

N E P A L

BHUTAN

○ Agra

Pushkar ○   ○ Jaipur

Ganges River

Prayag ○   ○ Varanasi

Bodhgaya ○

BANGLADESH

MYANMAR
(BURMA)

Kolkata ○

A r a b i a n

S e a

○ Mumbai

B a y

o f

B e n g a l

N

W — E

S

○ GOA

Bangalore ○   ○ Chennai

Key
■ Capital city
○ Other cities

0 ___ miles ___ 500
0 ___ kilometres ___ 500

I n d i a n   O c e a n

SRI
LANKA

◀ *India shares its
northern borders
with six countries:
Bangladesh,
Pakistan, Bhutan,
Nepal, China
and Myanmar
(Burma).*

Location in the world

India is located in south Asia and is the seventh largest country in the world. With a land area of more than 3 million sq km (1.1 million sq miles), it is one-third the size of the USA and more than 13 times the size of the UK. The shape of the country means that it has land borders only in the north. It is bordered by the Arabian Sea in the west, the Bay of Bengal in the east and the Indian Ocean in the south. Altogether it has 7,517 km (4,671 miles) of coastline. Off the south coast of India is the island of Sri Lanka, India's nearest neighbour by sea.

Long relationships

India has had relationships with other countries for many centuries, and the region has been invaded many times by armies from Asia, the Middle East and Europe. Each time this happened, the invading countries left their mark on India. For example, the most famous building in the country, the Taj Mahal, was built by the Mughal Emperor Shah Jahan. The Mughals, who came from Central Asia, ruled India between 1526 and 1761. Invading armies also took ideas from India back to their homelands, and this helped to spread Indian ideas around the world. Among these influences are the religions of Hinduism, Sikhism and Buddhism, which all began in India.

BASIC DATA

Official name: **Republic of India**	
Capital: **New Delhi**	
Size: **3,287,590 sq km (1,269,346 sq miles)**	
Population: **1,147,995,904**	
Currency: **Rupee**	

▼ *On the banks of the Yamuna River in Agra, the Taj Mahal stands as a symbol of India's Mughal past.*

A growing power

By 2008, India had the world's twelfth largest economy and experts believe that if it keeps growing at its current rate, India will be second only to China by 2050. Individuals and companies in India are also becoming globally significant. In 2008, four of the top 10 richest people in the world were Indians, and Indian companies such as Tata, which makes cars and computer software among other things, are now some of the largest in the world.

IT STARTED HERE

Planned cities

Archaeologists have found the remains of planned cities that date back more than 5,000 years in northern India and its modern-day neighbour Pakistan. It is thought that buildings from this time had sewage systems and running water.

The challenge of growth

India's population has more than doubled since 1970, and it is difficult to provide housing, food, water and energy for everyone. Healthcare, education and jobs are also needed, and it is in these areas that India struggles to keep pace. In global terms, then, India is both a winner and a loser, and one of its biggest challenges is to make sure that everyone benefits from its growing power.

▲ As India's population grows, more and more people are travelling to cities to work and live. Finding housing and other necessities for all these people can be difficult.

Landscapes and environment

India is a vast country with many different landscapes. The north has snow-capped mountains and in the west there are large, dry deserts where very little grows. In the middle of the country is farmland, and further south and east there are forests and swamps.

Holy rivers

Rivers play an important role in Indian life – they bring water for farming and provide transport for trade, but they are also important spiritually. The River Ganges, in the north, is considered holy by people who follow the Hindu religion. It is known by many Indians simply as *Maa Ganga*, which means 'Mother River'. Many towns and cities on the Ganges have *ghats* (steps) down to the river so that people can bathe there. The holiest of these cities is Varanasi, which attracts thousands of Hindu pilgrims every year, from all over the world.

▼ *The main* ghat *(step down to the river) in Varanasi, on the Ganges, is a sacred site for Hindus and is frequently visited by pilgrims.*

Industry and pollution

In parts of India, the rapid growth in industry and population has harmed the environment. The main damage has been caused by the use of India's natural resources and by pollution from human activities. Some of the problems have been caused by people clearing forests for building towns or to make room for farmland, but some damage has more international connections. The global drinks company Coca Cola, for example, has been criticized for causing water shortages in parts of India by using local water supplies for its bottling factories.

▲ *Traditional methods of clearing forests are still used in India – here an elephant is moving recently felled teak trees.*

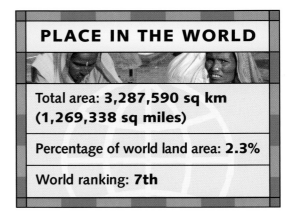

PLACE IN THE WORLD

Total area: **3,287,590 sq km (1,269,338 sq miles)**

Percentage of world land area: **2.3%**

World ranking: **7th**

Choking on air

In India's largest cities, transport, industries and households pump out a mix of smoke and chemicals that create some of the most polluted air in the world. It is estimated that around 530,000 people die from diseases caused by air pollution every year in India. India releases more of the greenhouse gas carbon dioxide into the atmosphere than any other country except the USA, China and Russia. However, India's large population means that carbon-dioxide emissions per person are much lower than in many other countries – in fact, India ranks 135th in the world in terms of carbon dioxide per person.

▶ *Rickshaws are the most convenient method of travelling on India's roads. In some places, gas-powered rickshaws are now used, to reduce traffic pollution.*

Protecting the environment

During the 1970s and 1980s, a number of local groups began to raise concerns about the damage being caused to India's environment. One of the most famous of these groups was the Chipko Movement, in which campaigners used peaceful methods to make their protest, such as hugging trees to stop them being chopped down. Several Indian states have banned or controlled logging as a result of the group's actions.

FAMOUS INDIANS

Vandana Shiva (b. 1952)

Vandana Shiva is a scientist and campaigner who is famous for speaking out against environmental destruction. She was a member of the Chipko Movement, and since then she has travelled the world to help other campaigners protect the environment and improve the status of women in society.

Wildlife and conservation

India is home to almost eight per cent of the world's mammal species, 12 per cent of fish species and 13 per cent of bird species, which means that protecting India's wildlife is important globally as well as locally. In the 1970s, the Indian government set up many national parks and protected areas as part of its national wildlife-conservation programme. By 2008, India had 96 national parks and 515 protected areas.

▼ *A Bengal tigress in the Bandavgarh National Park. The Indian government is committed to protecting India's tiger population from extinction.*

GLOBAL LEADER

Tiger protection
In 1973, the Indian government launched a conservation programme called 'Project Tiger'. At that time, India had fewer than 300 tigers left. Project Tiger set up a network of 27 reserves to protect tigers from poachers and other human activities. By 2004, the tiger population had increased to almost 1,600, which was nearly half the world total.

Population and migration

As home to one-sixth of all the people on Earth, India's population growth has a major influence on the world. If 100 people represented the total global population, then 17 would be from India, 20 would be from China and 4.5 from the USA.

PLACE IN THE WORLD

Population: **1,147,995,904**

Percentage of world total: **17%**

World ranking: **2nd**

Population explosion

Experts believe that by 2025, the population of India will pass that of China, although the rate of increase has slowed in recent years. Indian women today have an average of less than three children each, compared to six in the 1950s. The government has helped this reduction by introducing family planning and better healthcare. India's population is still growing, though, because almost a third of its people are under the age of 15. As these children grow up and start their own families, the population continues to increase.

▼ *Crowds waiting to board the train at New Delhi. More than 300 trains a day pass through this busy station.*

THE HOME OF...

Railways

The Indian railway system is the largest in Asia and one of the biggest employers in the world, with more than 1.54 million workers. Every day more than 11,000 trains carry people and goods around India, stopping at many of the 6,853 train stations.

Food crisis

One of the challenges of a growing population is being able to feed everyone. In the 1960s, there was a revolution in farming methods to try to increase food production – new types of rice and wheat were introduced, and more chemicals and water were used to improve their growth. Food production more than doubled and India avoided famine at the time, but despite this it is estimated that 340 million people in India still go to bed hungry every night. Many people think India needs a second revolution, using genetically modified (GM) crops, but some farmers, politicians and members of the general public are worried about the safety of GM food.

▲ *Women planting rice in a paddy field in Malappuram, southern India. India and China together produce more than half the world's rice.*

Indians abroad

In 2004, an estimated 20 million Indians were living overseas – almost the same as the population of Australia. South Africa, the USA, the UK and Canada all have large Indian communities, as people have been attracted to these wealthier countries by better jobs and higher incomes than those available in India. Despite moving away, most Indians maintain strong links with their families in India, including sending home money called 'remittances' to help them.

FAMOUS INDIANS

Kalpana Chawla (1962–2003)

Kalpana Chawla was the first Indian American to fly a space shuttle. Kalpana was born in Haryana, northern India, and she moved to the USA in 1984 to study at university. Following a career with NASA, Kalpana was killed in 2003 when the Space Shuttle *Columbia* exploded.

▼ *Young girls celebrate the Divali Festival of Lights in Auckland, New Zealand. As Indian people settle around the world, they take with them important cultural traditions.*

Super cities

India has three of the world's 20 most populated cities. Mumbai is the largest, with 19 million people, followed by Delhi with 15.9 million and then Kolkata with 14.8 million. New people arrive in these and other cities every day hoping to find good jobs, but in reality India's cities struggle to support the new migrants. People often end up living in areas of poor-quality housing known as slums. In Mumbai, around two-thirds of the population live in slums.

Removing the slums

The Indian government has tried to clear slums in a number of ways. Sometimes it has forced people to move back to the areas they came from, or it has demolished slums built on government land. The government has also spent a lot of money on building new, affordable housing that has proper water supplies and sewage systems. Despite this, India's slums continue to grow – a problem that is shared by other developing countries, including Brazil, Mexico and China.

▲ *Women living in a city-centre slum. The government is trying to reduce the number of people living in these areas by introducing new housing plans in cities and suburbs.*

GOING GLOBAL

Many Indians living abroad send most of the money they earn home to family and friends as remittances. In 2007, an incredible US$27 billion was sent back to India from Indians living overseas.

Culture and lifestyles

Modern India is a melting-pot of cultures – old and new – from around the world. Ancient temples bustle with people offering prayers, while on the buildings next to them there are neon signs advertising Japanese electronic goods or Western fast food.

Global religions

Many religions are worshipped in India, including Hinduism, Buddhism, Christianity, Sikhism and Islam. Hinduism, Buddhism and Sikhism were founded in India, and more than 920 million Indians are Hindus – 80.5 per cent of the population. Every 12 years, more than 70 million Hindus (more than the population of the UK) make a pilgrimage to Prayag, in the north of the country, to worship together. This is called the Maha Kumbh Mela and it is the world's largest gathering of people.

▼ *Hindu pilgrims gathering to bathe at the Maha Kumbh Mela in Prayag, northern India. As well as bathing, pilgrims pray, worship and discuss their religion.*

Buddhism in India

Buddhism was founded in Bodhgaya, northern India during the fifth century BCE. Buddhists from all over the world make pilgrimages to India and around eight million Indians today are Buddhists.

▼ *Buddhist monks praying under the bodhy (fig) tree in Bodhgaya, the birthplace of Buddhism.*

Bollywood

India's film industry is known as Bollywood and it is the largest in the world. Bollywood makes over 800 films a year (twice as many as Hollywood) and sells an amazing 14 million movie tickets every day. Most Bollywood films are musicals, with singing and dancing. Many Bollywood films are in the Hindi language, but more and more are being made in English because of their great popularity outside India, with the UK having one of the largest audiences. The themes of the films are also showing Western influences and are becoming more like Hollywood movies.

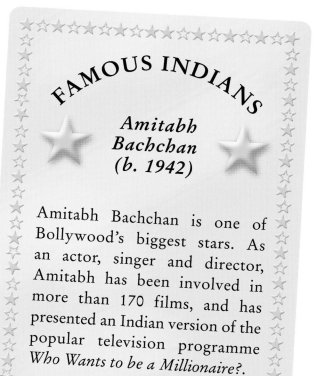

FAMOUS INDIANS

Amitabh Bachchan (b. 1942)

Amitabh Bachchan is one of Bollywood's biggest stars. As an actor, singer and director, Amitabh has been involved in more than 170 films, and has presented an Indian version of the popular television programme *Who Wants to be a Millionaire?*.

Different childhoods

Children growing up in India can lead very different lives depending on how wealthy their parents are and where they live. In cities, children may live in overcrowded apartments or in slums where there is little space to play. In rural areas, houses are more spread out but they may not have electricity or running water. Children have more space to play, but they may have to help their parents on the family farm. Board games and cricket are especially popular among Indian children. For those who can afford it, Western interests such as computer games are becoming increasingly popular.

◀ *India is globally famous for cricket. Makeshift cricket pitches can be seen on beaches or in the streets all over the country.*

Sporting pastimes

Playing or watching sport is a favourite pastime in India, and the country is famous around the world for its achievements in cricket. India won the Cricket World Cup in 1983 and was runner-up in 2003. Any empty space, whether a beach, field or city alleyway is used by children practising cricket, and during a big game, large cities come to a near standstill. In 2010, New Delhi will host the Commonwealth Games, which will see 4,500 athletes from 71 countries take part in more than 250 different sporting events.

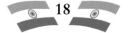

IT STARTED HERE

Yoga

The ancient Indian meaning of the word yoga is 'to control'. For centuries yoga has been used by Indians as a way of controlling breathing, and helping the mind and the body. It is now popular around the world as a method of fitness and relaxation.

Indian culture overseas

As Indian people have migrated around the world, they have taken their culture with them. Indian food, for example, is now extremely popular in many countries. In the UK, Indian food (especially curry) has become the nation's favourite dish, with more than 2.5 million people visiting Indian restaurants every week.

GLOBAL LEADER

Tea cultivation

India produces 12 per cent of the world's tea and, together with China, it is a global leader in tea cultivation. In the UK alone, people drink 165 million cups of tea every day!

▼ *A tea picker collecting leaves for drying on a tea plantation in Assam, southern India. India is famous for its tea, which is sold all over the world.*

Economy and trade

By 2008, India's economy was the twelfth largest in the world and the third largest in Asia, after Japan and China. This growth is changing how people work and what they do, as well as affecting the relationships India has with the rest of the world.

PLACE IN THE WORLD

Value of economy:
US$1,069,427,000,000

Percentage of world total: **2%**

World ranking: **12th**

Changing economy

Agriculture has always been important to the Indian economy, and the farming industry still employs around 60 per cent of all workers. Over the last 25 years, however, new industries have developed, most notably computer and software development. India's retail (shopping) industry has also grown quickly, as people with higher incomes have more money to spend. Service jobs like this employ almost 30 per cent of all workers today, compared to only 17 per cent in 1990.

▼ *Women selling fruit and vegetables at a road side stall in Jaipur. Small stalls like this are an important way of making a living.*

Outsourcing

India is now a popular destination for 'outsourcing' – when companies outside India hire Indian companies to do some of their call-centre and administration work. Because wages are much lower in India, a worker there can cost less than half as much as a worker in Europe or the USA. As skills and incomes have increased in India, Indian software companies like Infosys and Tata are now outsourcing work themselves to countries such as Brazil, Poland, Portugal and even the UK and USA.

▶ *Call-centre workers, like these in Bangalore, provide telephone support for companies from all over the world. Many big companies in North America and Europe outsource work to Indian companies.*

GLOBAL LEADER

Medical tourism

Each year, India welcomes more than 150,000 people who travel there for medical treatment from its highly qualified medical staff. They can provide treatments such as eye surgery, hip replacements and cosmetic surgery at much lower costs than in Europe or the USA. By 2012, India could earn over US$1 billion a year from medical tourism.

New partnerships

Together with Brazil, Russia and China, India is one of the four countries that experts believe will become global superpowers by 2050. India is developing new business and partnerships with these countries, and is also making trade deals with them. In 2006, India and China agreed to double the amount of trade between the two countries by 2010.

Indian businesses

Many Indian businesses are now so successful that they have begun to buy companies in other countries. For example, in 2007, Tata Steel bought the British-Dutch steel company Corus, to become the world's fifth largest steel company. In 2008, Tata Cars bought the global car brands Jaguar and Land Rover from their American owners, Ford.

The tourist industry

India's tourist industry is another way in which India has growing global links. There are now many flights to India from other countries in Asia, as well as from Europe and the USA.

IT'S A FACT!

In 2008, Tata announced it was going to produce a new car called the 'Nano'. The Nano would sell for only US$2,500 – much less than cars made by other manufacturers. The Nano is a symbol of India's growing power in key global markets.

▼ *Tourists taking a camel ride in Pushkar, northern India. Many tourists come to India to experience the country's different cultures.*

Tourist origins and destinations

The number of tourists visiting India doubled between 1996 and 2006 to 4.4 million. Most tourists come from the UK, USA, Canada, France and Germany, and between them they spent US$8,885 million in 2006. Most tourists go to just a few locations, such as the beaches of Goa or the 'golden triangle' of Delhi, Jaipur and Agra, which includes many of India's finest palaces.

Child labour and poverty

India still faces some serious challenges. About a quarter of the population lives in poverty. Families are forced to send their children out to work to help earn money – about five per cent of children in India aged between seven and 14 have to work. Most of these (about 73 per cent) work in farming and almost all of them have had to give up school. Some children work in factories, producing manufactured goods such as clothes that are sold in Europe or the USA. There have been campaigns in many countries against child labour, and now a lot of factories have controls to prevent children working in them.

> ▶ *There are still some factories – such as this match factory – that employ children. Many organizations in India, and around the world, are calling for an end to child labour.*

THE HOME OF...

The Taj Mahal

In 2007, the Taj Mahal was voted a new Wonder of the World. More than 100 million people around the world took part in the vote. Every year, more than four million people visit the site, making it one of the most visited buildings in the world.

Government and politics

India is home to one of the oldest civilizations on Earth, and it has had local systems of government in place for centuries. By the seventeenth century, though, European powers had seized control of India, and it only regained its independence in 1947.

Independent India

Following independence, the new leaders of India, Mahatma Gandhi and Jawaharlal Nehru, wanted to bring India's many different people together under a single national government. India was divided into 28 states and seven union territories, which today have the power to make decisions over such things as healthcare and education.

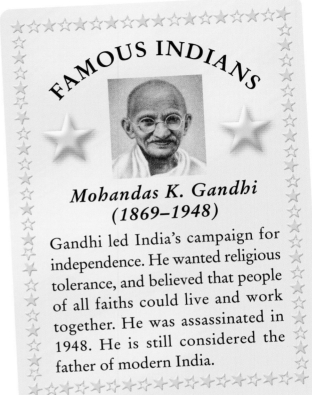

FAMOUS INDIANS

**Mohandas K. Gandhi
(1869–1948)**

Gandhi led India's campaign for independence. He wanted religious tolerance, and believed that people of all faiths could live and work together. He was assassinated in 1948. He is still considered the father of modern India.

◀ *Ensuring all adults can vote is an important aspect of India's political system. Here, a government official shows tea-plantation workers in northern India how to vote using special voting machines.*

The world's biggest democracy

Everyone over the age of 18 is allowed to vote in India. In 2008, more than 670 million people were eligible to vote, which makes it the world's biggest democracy. Elections in India are held every five years and voters can choose from hundreds of different parties. Because up to 35 per cent of the adult population cannot read or write, special electronic voting machines have been introduced, which use images instead of words. India's prime minister is elected by the winning party, and a president is elected by members of the state and national governments every five years.

▲ *India's Minister of Commerce and Industry, Kamal Nath, shakes hands with World Trade Organization's Director General, Pascal Lamy, following trade talks in Switzerland.*

IT'S A FACT!

India is a member of many of the world's largest and most powerful organizations, including the United Nations (UN), the World Trade Organization (WTO), the World Bank and the International Monetary Fund (IMF).

A world leader?

As a future global superpower, India wants to be a part of the group of nations that are responsible for keeping world peace. There have been calls for India to be a member of the United Nations Security Council, which decides international action if war breaks out. By 2050, India – together with Brazil, Russia and China – will have combined economies that are larger than the rest of the world. These countries are known as BRIC nations, based on the first letters of their names.

GOING GLOBAL

In 2007, India sent the world's first all-female peacekeeping force to Liberia. More than 100 women were sent in to help rebuild Liberia's police force, which was destroyed after years of war. It was hoped that the all-women force would promote better relations between men and women in Liberia.

▼ *The world's first all-female Indian peacekeeping force arrives in Liberia in 2007 to work alongside the Liberian national police.*

▲ *Crowds cheer at the daily flag-lowering ceremony at the Indian-Pakistan border, before the 2008 terrorist attacks worsened the relationship between the two countries.*

PLACE IN THE WORLD

Number of people who can vote:
671,524,934

Percentage of world total: **15.2%**

World ranking: **1st**

Tensions with Pakistan

Despite good relationships with many countries, India has had problems with its closest neighbour, Pakistan. The reason for this is the disputed ownership of Kashmir (which is situated on the border) and access to natural water supplies. Over the last 60 years, fighting has broken out between India and Pakistan a number of times, but in 2004 an uneasy peace was established. In 2008, a series of terrorist attacks was carried out in Mumbai, and hundreds of Indians were killed or injured. The Indian government believed that the terrorists were from Pakistan, and relations between the two countries worsened again.

India in 2020

As India approaches 2020, its position in the world will continue to change. To be a global superpower, India will have to make sure that it is recognized as a powerful nation, but it will also have to make sure its people are properly cared for. This will mean addressing many of the problems faced at home as well as abroad.

More people

If the population continues to grow at its current rate, by 2020 there will be 300 million more people living in India. To cope with this increased population, India's cities will continue to grow. With more people to feed, India will have to think about water supplies and new food sources, either imported from foreign countries or produced in a different way in India itself. India will have to increase its use of renewable energy sources, such as wind, solar and wave power. India is seeking to become a world leader in wind power, and is already the fifth biggest wind-power producer. In this respect, it is well on the way to addressing future energy problems.

◀ *Young women collecting water in north-east India. Ensuring good water for all will be a challenge for the Indian government as the population continues to increase.*

Working together

Strong relationships with other countries will be very important for India's future. Building on the trade agreements it already has will be important to ensure that imports of oil and minerals continue. India's current biggest trading partners, China and the USA, will be even more important in 2020. Strong relationships with the other BRIC nations will support India's role as an important industrial nation, and many countries will choose to outsource more and more work to India and other developing nations.

India in the world

With such a big share of the global population, the ways in which Indian people live, work and enjoy their free time will have an increasing impact on the rest of the world. Lifestyle choices such as what food people eat, whether they drive to work and how much water they use will continue to not only shape India, but the rest of the world as well.

▼ *Increasing renewable energy sources, like this wind farm in Kaiyrathry, is an important part of India's plans for the future.*

Glossary

BRIC nations the countries that are expected to become the most powerful in the world in the next few years. The name comes from the initials of Brazil, Russia, India and China.

Buddhism a religion that follows the teachings of Buddha (c. 563-483 BCE), and involves studying wisdom, meditation and following an ethical code.

call centre usually an office where people make and receive telephone calls and emails on behalf of a business. Not all companies have their own call centres.

child labour where children go to work, often instead of going to school.

Chipko Movement a political campaign that attempted to stop trees being cut down for industry.

Christianity a religion that follows the teachings of Jesus Christ.

Commonwealth Games a sporting event held every four years for countries that were once part of the Commonwealth of Nations.

conservation looking after the natural environment and wildlife.

democracy a system where people have the power to choose who governs the country by voting.

economy the financial system of a country or region, including how much money is made from the production and sale of goods and services.

emissions gases that are given off during industrial processes or by vehicles.

Hinduism an ancient religion founded in India. Hindus believe in one god called Brahmin who takes on different forms, referred to as deities not gods.

import to bring in goods or materials from a foreign country for sale.

independence the process of India becoming its own country and no longer being part of the British Empire.

Islam a religion with belief in one god (Allah) and his last prophet, Muhammad.

migrants people who move from one place to another to live or work.

minerals natural rocks that come from the ground.

outsourcing where companies are hired to do work on behalf of another company.

religious tolerance a situation where people from all religions respect one another's point of view.

renewable energy sources energy sources that can be replaced easily such as solar power from the sun, wind power and wave power from the sea.

retail the selling of goods and services.

Sikhism a religion founded in India around 600 years ago.

Further information

Books

Changing World: India
by Rob Bowden
(Franklin Watts, 2008)

Countries in the News: India
by Anita Ganeri
(Franklin Watts, 2009)

India
by Manini Chatterjee and
Anita Roy
(DK Eyewitness Books, 2002)

India (Festivals and Food)
by Mike Hirst
(Wayland, 2006)

Teens in India: Global Connections
by Lori Shores
(Compass Point Books, 2007)

The Changing Face of India
by David Cumming
(Wayland, 2001)

Websites

http://www.hinduonnet.com/
India's English-language newspaper online.

**http://news.bbc.co.uk/1/hi/world/south_asia/
country_profiles/1154019.stm**
BBC News online country profile.

**http://cyberschoolbus.un.org/infonation/
index.asp?id=356**
United Nations website information about
all countries.

http://www.incredibleindia.org/
India tourism website.

*Every effort has been made by the publisher to ensure
that these websites contain no inappropriate or offensive
material. However, because of the nature of the Internet,
it is impossible to guarantee that the contents of these sites
will not be altered. We strongly advise that Internet access
is supervised by a responsible adult.*

Index

Numbers in **bold** indicate pictures

Teddington
Library